T0381319

In My Room

Maestro

To order additional copies of this book, contact:
Xlibris Corporation
1-888-795-4274
www.Xlibris.com
Orders@Xlibris.com

Haiku: "My Arrival"

In July it's hot!,

Grass grows, flowers at full bloom,

In Summer, I came.

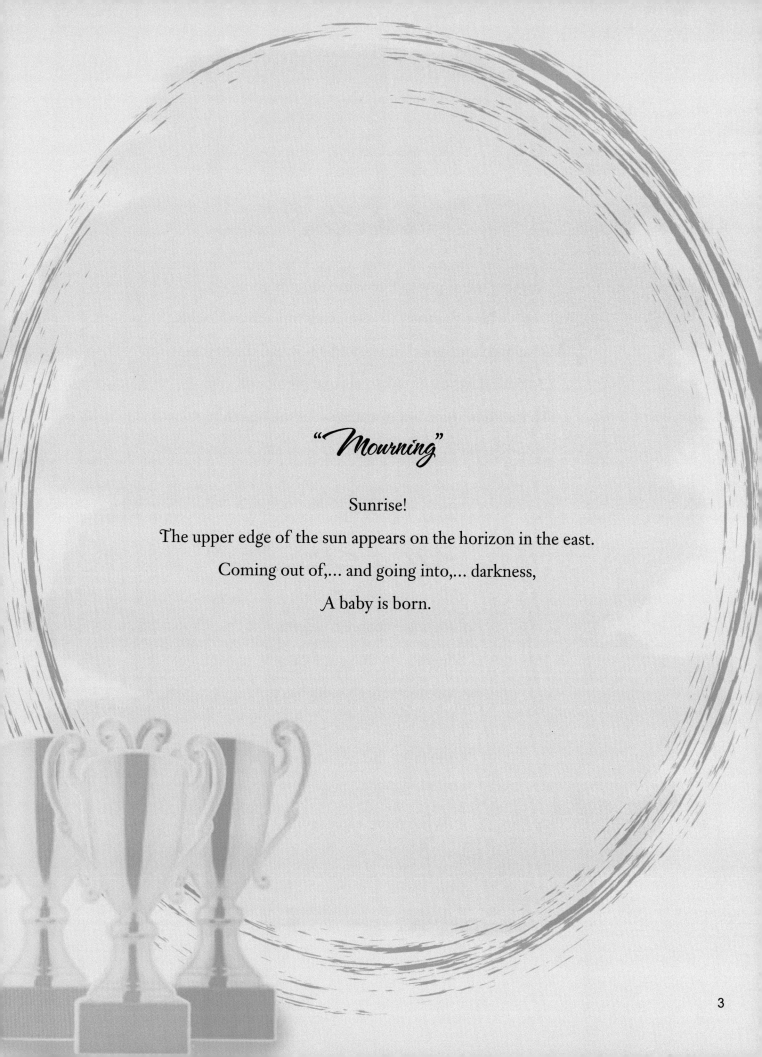

"*Mourning*"

Sunrise!

The upper edge of the sun appears on the horizon in the east.

Coming out of,... and going into,... darkness,

A baby is born.

"Another Day"

Another day is gone, The same thing is going on..

At least we have the past, to reminisce sit back and laugh.

We've had some good times, and a few bad times too.

My mind has captured an eternal picture of you.

That's not so bad, but nothing's like the real thing.

Maybe one day we'll be back together, you can be my queen.

"His & Hers"

In the low income residents,

She says anything she can,

He says no more than he has to.

In the suburbs,

She talks and he listens.

In the mansions,

What more can I say?

"A Prayer"

Forgive me, I am but a child,

Though trying to walk and stand tall.

As my strength begins to weaken

Catch me when I fall,

Because I adhere to some of your teachings,

But for temptation, I cannot!,.....

Adhere to them all.

"A World Without a Superman"

A world without a superman, is all but under the sand.

No one to say to the people, Yes, you can!

No one to plan.

No one to take a stand and fight the bad man.

No one to escape plan, when you can't take a stand.

No one to believe in.

No one to take on the wars that regular guys can't win.

A little superman lies within all men.

Some just have to look a little further within.

A world without a superman is a world without men.

"Epic"

Life itself is,

Understanding also is,

The Heavens are,

Mathematical,

Fluid Motion,

Grace,

Tales of a Quest,

A heroic journey,

Laughter,

The essence of comedy,

The rhythm of dance,

Oceanic Movements,

Sexual Chemistry,

The structure of the mind,

Your genetic makeup,

You, yourself,

Me, myself,

Epic!

"Fall In"

I couldn't get in where I fit in,

So I fell in where I was caught.

I fell in like a platoon of soldiers on the march.

Left, Right, Left, Watch your step,

Life's a game of dirty hearts.

Get in where you fit in.

I fell in like the rain,

Cold and scattered.

"Fierce Lightning"

Lightning is frightening; you see it and run,

Muscles tighten from the striking, and thunders like a gun,

That's blasting, or cannons exploding eardrums.

The splashing of rain, pouring downward it comes,

In like the night, or a thief as he runs,

In pursuit or in fright from police and there horns.

A lesson from lightening, not one to forget,

Could not escape fate, cause Zeus was too quick.

No matter, tall tale or fable, lightening is fierce.

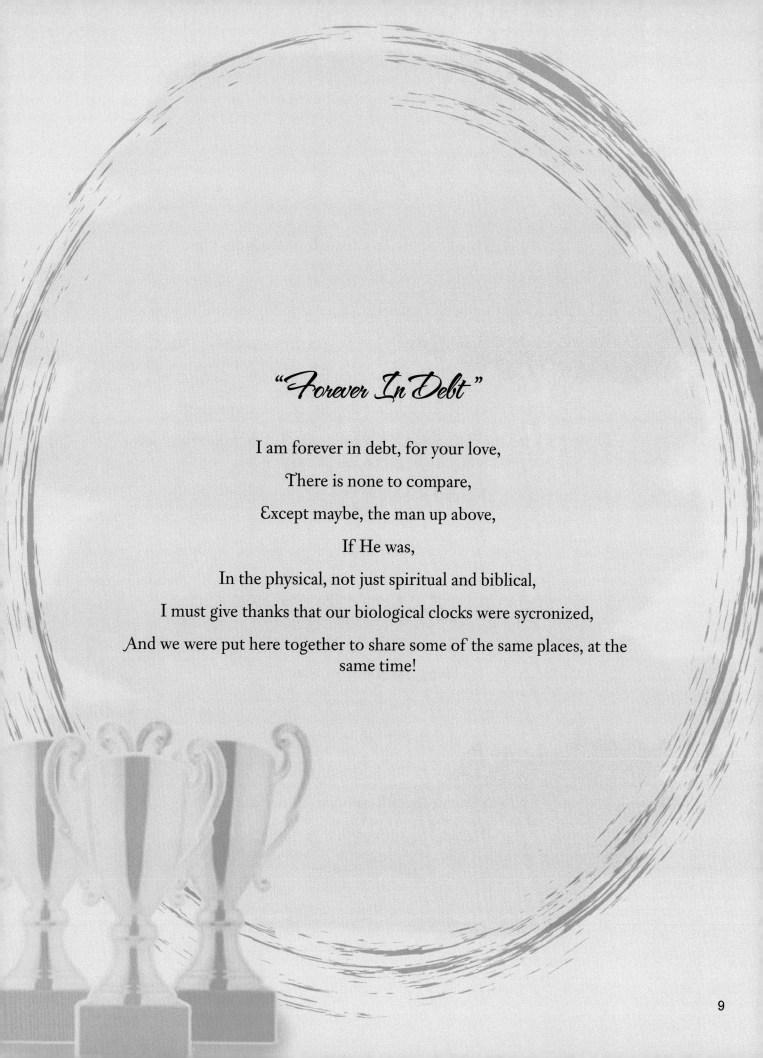

"Forever In Debt"

I am forever in debt, for your love,

There is none to compare,

Except maybe, the man up above,

If He was,

In the physical, not just spiritual and biblical,

I must give thanks that our biological clocks were sycronized,

And we were put here together to share some of the same places, at the same time!

"Gift"

Precious gift, what a lift, in a rush, how the time slips,

These words to you I'd never say, how happy I was on that day.

Feelings hurt, but mine don't work, as they should, but still I'm good.

As for you, my love is always true, I know you often question things I do.

I won't say, for you I'll skate through fire while covered in gas,

Or after taking an oil bath, maybe just to make you laugh.

Laughter warms the soul, lies soon come to an end, but the truth never
gets old.

And the truth of the matter is I love you more than my own big toe.

"I Am.....Not"

I hear, but I do not hear.

I see, but I do not see.

I feel, but I do not feel.

I think, but I do not think.

And yet, if you are still trying to figure me out,

Here is the answer to this riddle,

I Am.....Not!

"In My Room"

Thoughts caught upon my wall, dreams and wishes contrived, big and small.

Thunderings and bolts, demons and spirits great, mountain peaks, plateau's and lakes.

Galaxy's of stars, tragedies filled with blood and scars.

A little love, hate and envy, With a bitterness that is, if not more, just as depressing as unsweetened tea.

Riddles, poems, rhymes, books, cowboys and Indians, robbers, gangsters, thieves, crooks.

Sex, crime, lust, lies and passion, lady's outfits, war boots, men's gear and designer fashion.

Rock and Roll, Silky Soul, Oldie Gold and sweet Love Classics,

When combined, the melodies, the rhythm's and the tunes, it makes magic.....In My Room!

"*Maturity*"

A step up! A switch up from left to right.
Aging! A changing, from day to night.
Climaxing! Growing up, from land to flight,
Boys to men, dark to bright.

Seeing things for what they really are,
Transportation, fuel, indentures, a car isn't just a car.
Are your friends who they say they are?
Ex-girlfriend, a junkie? Basketball buddy, a convict? Nerdy friend, a star?

Yesterdays gone by, they matter no more,
But folly and mistakes of a youth, to bear, what a chore.
Laugh now, cry later they said, but we had to explore.
From birds nest to wings of eagles we soar. With growth, never to implore.

If you stumble, and do have to beg and crawl, remember from your fall!
That's maturity., Once recognized, cherish it. It doesn't come to us all.

"Maybe"

Maybe we're under reconstruction.

These a theories for those who fear spontaneous combustion.

Maybe we're reincarnates.

Since everything evolves, maybe we did come from apes.

Maybe life is just a hard lesson.

Maybe our so-called leaders need to quit guessing.

Maybe I should kill a few folks,

Then maybe they would laugh when I told a joke,

Even when it's not funny,

You know how people treat those with a lot of money.

Maybe it was meant to be.

Maybe what you get is more than what you just see.

Maybe Angels are watching over us,

And it's a pretty good show.

Maybe I'll never know.

Maybe justice is really blind.

Or Maybe, you'll reap what you sow.

Maybe!

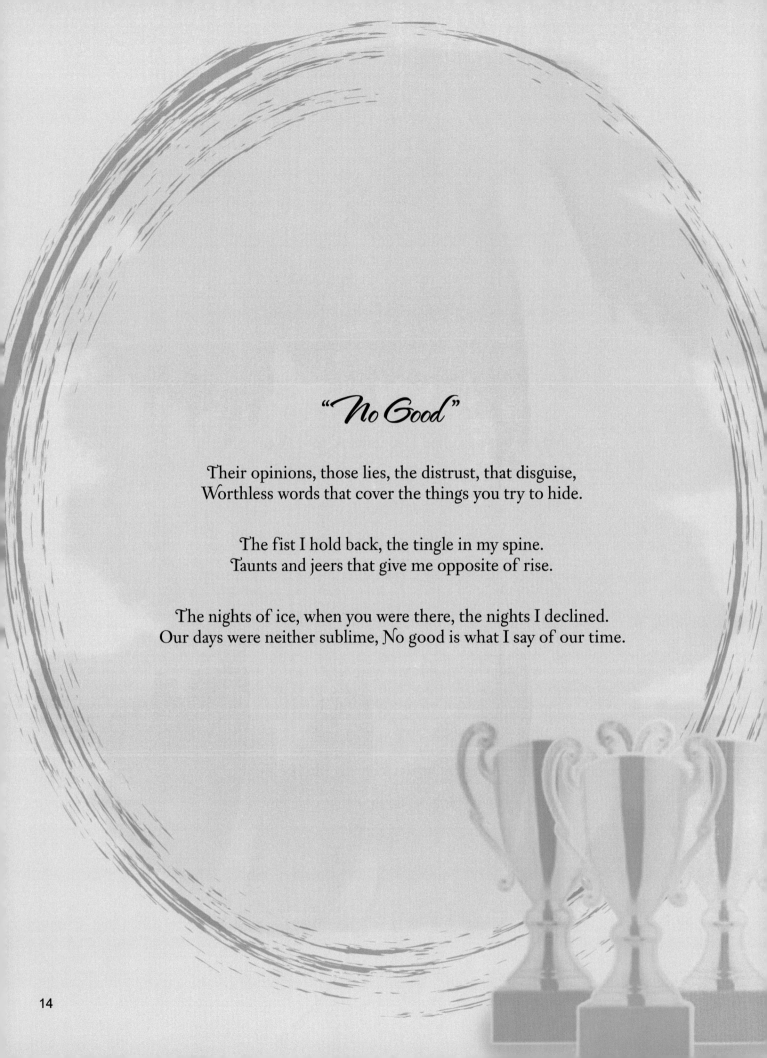

"No Good"

Their opinions, those lies, the distrust, that disguise,
Worthless words that cover the things you try to hide.

The fist I hold back, the tingle in my spine.
Taunts and jeers that give me opposite of rise.

The nights of ice, when you were there, the nights I declined.
Our days were neither sublime, No good is what I say of our time.

"No Room for Mistakes"

I've searched through the Lows and the Highs, in search for just the right place,

I got an email address, PO Box and a combination lock box on the inside of my padlock safe.

It's not in the most kindest, most peaceful, man's mind, or a low down dirty rotten heart full of hate,

It's like driving down a bridge and feeling the pads give away, by the hesitation of the tires reaction to the breaks.

While searching through closets, couches, under rugs, cabinets, behind doors and even under a vase,

Toy boxes, old cigar boxes, VHS, Memorex, and cassette tapes, the manager had no space,

When you feel like returning to retrieve something that you've left behind, because life where you are is not great,

Remember that, in future, past or present, there are no room for mistakes!

"Pain is Understanding"

When a situation involves pain,

You learn to think twice,

Or not to do it again.

Or.....at least that its' results are in pain.

Pain and consequences,

Even a child knows,

that with bad behavior comes painful blows.

Some people, cause pain and harm on themselves,

Which also gives pain to relatives, friends and mothers.

While some, like to inflict pain elsewhere,

Because they enjoy the pain of others.

Pain of Lovers'!

They say it's the worst and could kill.

That would explain,

Why, I am painless still.

"Slave Baby"

Seed sown, never to be grown,

Love unknown until one's grown.

Captured, as the thoughts in my head,

As the brain in my skull,

And as the bones in my body,

And a torch has been lit on the walls in the chambers of my heart.

But who knows?,

I am but a slave baby.

Yet, not through physical bondage,

But because of my beliefs, dreams and aspirations,

I have been out-casted and held captive in the spirit realm,

Where souls cry out, but no one hears,

Sculptures of pain appear as flickering images in the darkness,

Where the human flesh is useless,

Only used as a façade to bring seconds of pleasure,

or of tales of a life before.

My only desire, wish and prayer is, ...to be set free,

But who knows?

I am but a slave baby.

"Slow Motion"

Finding the wills to keep coasting, as a boat with a sail does on the ocean,

A change in life for the better is what I'm hoping.

Good things don't last long, though they do stop by and poke in,

For such, the windows always open, and so is the door.

A chore to explore, because things are always foreclosing,

Then I must move on, Can't just sit around loathing, corroding, moping.

Implanted in the mist of life's cycle, intertwined with death, just as father time.

When it's time for time to cease, to my knowledge at least, soon after it reaches it's peak.

Even then I will be, drifting through life's ills as a boat with a sail does on the ocean.

As a tiger prowls the grass, not giving his prey the slightest notion,

I guess that it is also best that I take my strides in a calm, cool, and easy,

Slow Motion!

"Something"

You can't make something out of nothing.

And, the only way to get nothing from something, is to leave it alone.

Nothing from nothing leaves nothing.

And, anything is better than nothing.

Something added to something, is really something,

And, It's always good to have something.

If you think you can take nothing and turn it into something,

I wish you the best of luck.

But, don't turn from something to nothing,

Because, it's a trap that will ensnare you every time.

It's better to be caught with nothing than something.

But, it's better to be found with something than nothing.

"The Fate of a Cold Heart"

I discovered while sitting in a room alone in the dark,

The fate of a cold heart,

Relationships find their end, even quicker than their start.

Friends who bring suitcases for the long haul, they too, shortly depart.

The opposite sex plays, but does not stay.

The ice cream that I take in is not this cold, bowl after bowl,

Who needs ice, if you could taste this soul.

Halt! Warning!, do not cross that bridge!

There is a very high toll.

Somehow they know, so they go, but I wish they would stay.

I suffered so long from the fate of a cold heart,

That, just as my shadow I became dark.

Yet too much strength to despair, with a flick of light,

To my relief, I looked back to find that my shadow was still there.

As for now, though I sit alone in the dark,

There is still hope, even for

The fate of a cold heart.

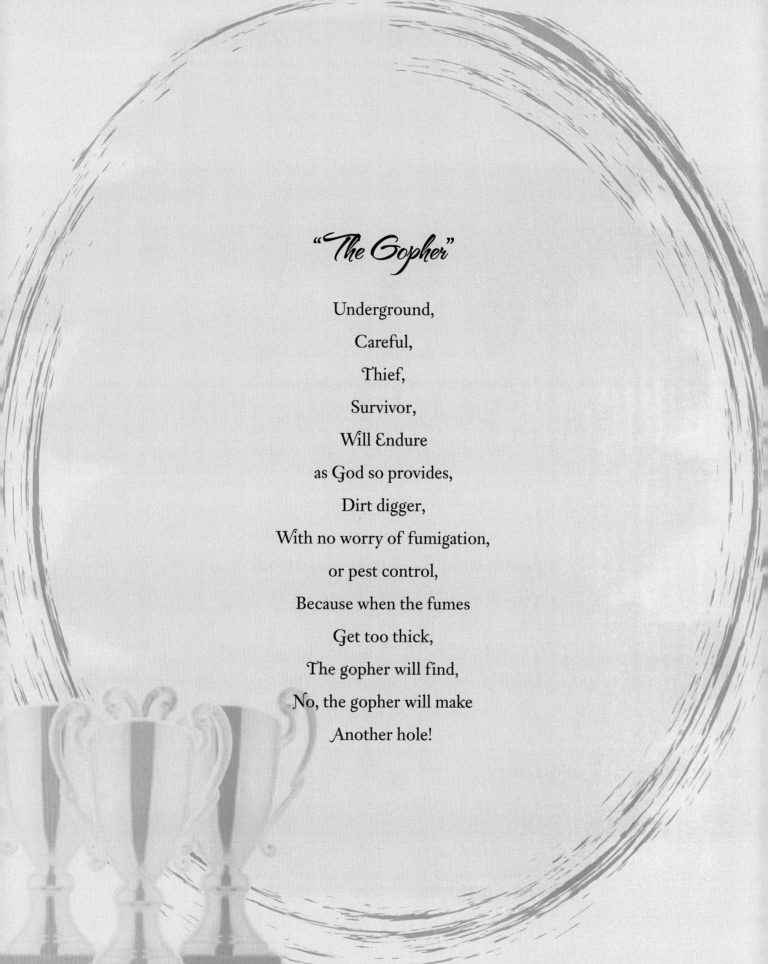

"The Gopher"

Underground,

Careful,

Thief,

Survivor,

Will Endure

as God so provides,

Dirt digger,

With no worry of fumigation,

or pest control,

Because when the fumes

Get too thick,

The gopher will find,

No, the gopher will make

Another hole!

"Times"

For times gone by, I set out and cry,

Not literally, but it has misted my eye.

As Lords, Kings and soldiers die.

For, when is the time to tell me why?

For days and times left behind.

I stretch my memory, then jog my mind.

Good times, bad times, Great times, Cruel times.

Questions unanswered! What were the signs?

For in these days and times, a blind man struggles,

It seems that love doesn't love you as in the times of others.

"Visions Blurred"

Let me show you something, Listen to me good my son,

I have bullet wounds because the man was testing his gun.

And when the world realized that I was an innocent man,

But at the time of the shooting, an innocent child.

They all said in unison, we must kill him now!

"Price"

Souls burned, to late to overturn the verdict.

Die, Die!, was the cry and everyone heard it.

When it's time to repay the man that was murdered,

This is the price.

"Weasel"

As I sit here about to die, as a weasel after rolling around on a back tire.

As I await for my time to expire, I look upon a passerbyer,

Who says, it is just a weasel, no sir, but you're a liar.

A weasel is but, a survivor.

"What is Right"

What is right?, we ask a world who kills dreams.

What is there really to do, if someone killed Dr. Martin Luther King?

Jr. that is, because he was someone's son.

What is there really to do, Why would we run?

What is right? We ask a world so cold.

What is there really to do, if you murder the young and put away the old?

There is no right, a man can only belong, but never win.

So, what is there rally to do, but try and fit in?

"*Sunset*"

Maybe later, not just yet.

I'm still playing, though I mustn't forget,

That at the end of the day,

The sun will set.

*A*s promised with this entry, author MAESTRO, who gave us his first novel, "The Working Cla$$" has now given us a collection of fruitful poetry that he hopes will keep on giving for years to come, but you be the judge.

Printed in the United States
by Baker & Taylor Publisher Services